A World of Field Trips

Going to a Stadium

Rebecca Rissman

www.raintreepublishers.co.uk

Visit our website to find out
more information about
Raintree books.

To order:

☎ Phone 0845 6044371
🖹 Fax +44 (0) 1865 312263
🖥 Email myorders@raintreepublishers.co.uk

Customers from outside the UK please telephone +44 1865 312262

Raintree is an imprint of Capstone Global Library Limited, a
company incorporated in England and Wales having its registered
office at 7 Pilgrim Street, London, EC4V 6LB – Registered
company number: 6695582.

Edited by Rebecca Rissman, Dan Nunn, and Catherine Veitch
Designed by Richard Parker
Picture research by Tracy Cummins
Originated by Capstone Global Library Ltd
Printed and bound in China by Leo Paper Products Ltd

ISBN 978 1 406 23520 3
16 15 14 13 12 11
10 9 8 7 6 5 4 3 2 1

British Library Cataloguing in Publication Data
Rissman, Rebecca.
Going to a stadium. -- (World of field trips)
796'.068-dc22

Acknowledgements
We would like to thank the following for permission to reproduce
photographs: Corbis pp. 6 (© Redlink), 13 (© Rolf Vennenbernd/
epa, 16 (© Kelly-Mooney Photography); Getty Images pp. 5
(Gage), 12 (Hisham Ibrahim), 15 (GOH CHAI HIN/AFP),
17 (Stephen Green/MLB Photos), 18 (Chris Graythen), 21,
23a (Kevork Djansezian), 23b (Stephen Green/MLB Photos);
Shutterstock pp. 4 (© Marek Pawluczuk), 7 (© fstockfoto), 8
© Neale Cousland), 9 (© Matt Trommer), 10 (© J. Henning
Buchholz), 11 (© Eric Broder Van Dyke), 14 (© sunxuejun), 19
(© Christopher Halloran), 20 (© L. Kragt Bakker), 22 (© Ffooter),
23c (© fstockfoto).

Front cover photograph of fans cheering the South African
National Soccer Team at the Atteridgeville stadium in Pretoria,
South Africa reproduced with permission of Getty Images (Per-
Anders Pettersson). Back cover photograph of a tennis stadium
reproduced with permission of Shutterstock (© Neale Cousland).

Every effort has been made to contact copyright holders of any
material reproduced in this book. Any omissions will be rectified
in subsequent printings if notice is given to the publisher.

Contents

Field trips

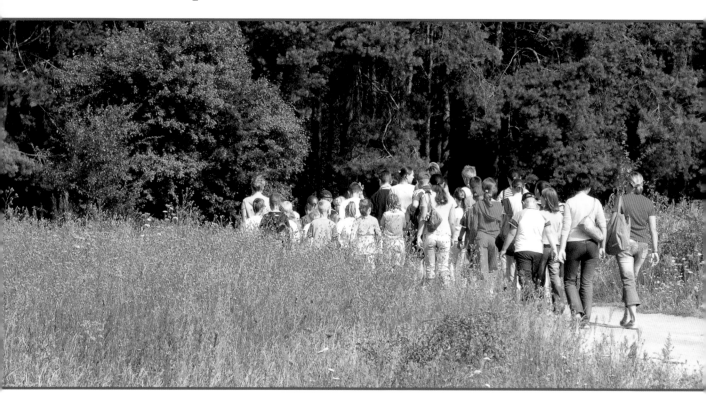

People go on field trips to see new places.

People go on field trips to learn new things.

Field trip to a stadium

Some people go on field trips
to stadiums.

A stadium is a place where people go to watch sport.

Stadiums have seats for people to watch sport.

Stadiums have fields for players to play on.

Different stadiums

Some stadiums are indoors.

The players stay dry in bad weather!

Some stadiums are outdoors.

The players feel the wind
and sunshine.

metal

Some stadiums are made of metal.

This stadium has a metal top.

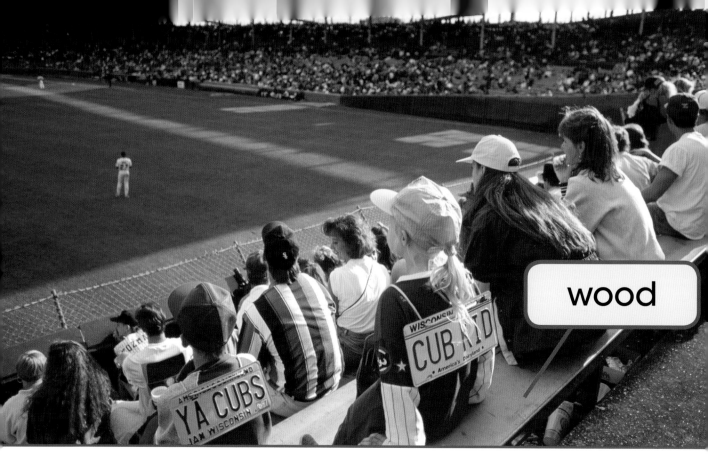

wood

Some stadiums are made of wood.

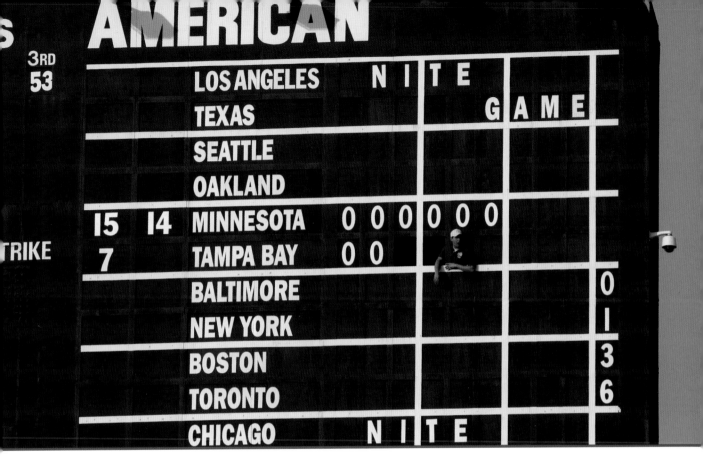

This stadium has a wooden scoreboard.

Some stadiums are very big.

This big stadium has a race track.

How should you behave at a stadium?

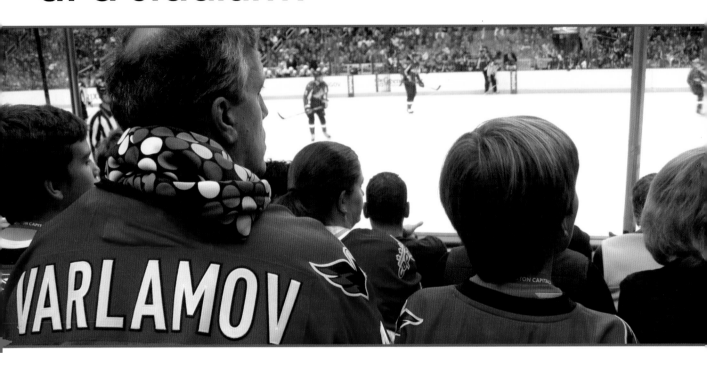

Always stay with an adult at a stadium.

You can cheer loudly for your team!

What do you think?

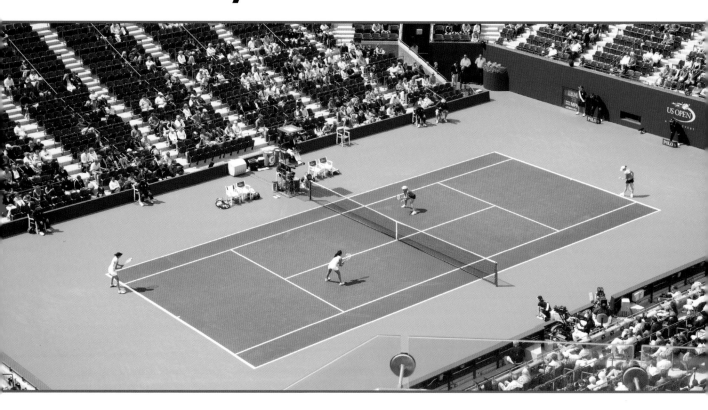

What kind of stadium is this?

Look on page 24 for the answer.

Picture glossary

cheer shout for a person or a team to succeed

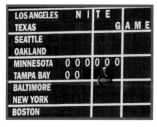

scoreboard part of a stadium that shows how many points each person or team has earned

stadium place where people gather to watch sport events

Index

Notes for parents and teachers

Before reading
Explain to children that a field trip is a short visit to a new place, and that it often takes place during a school day. Ask children if they have ever taken a field trip. Tell children that stadiums are where sporting events are held. Ask if any children play sport. Make a list of the sports they play on the board, and then guide children in a discussion about the different types of stadiums they may play in.

After reading
- Ask each child to draw a picture of a stadium, and then show it to the classroom. Ask the children to tell the class about their stadium, what types of sport could be played there, and if it has any special features.

Answer to page 22
It is a stadium where tennis is played.